To Phil Straw

with special thanks for your unflagging support and friendship from beginning to end

Thank you to the many friends who helped,
especially Miren, Haydn and David

Also by Jeannie Baker:

Belonging • *The Hidden Forest* • *Home in the Sky* • *Mirror* • *Millicent*
The Story of Rosy Dock • *Where the Forest Meets the Sea* • *Window*
www.jeanniebaker.com

First published 2016 by Walker Books Ltd, 87 Vauxhall Walk, London SE11 5HJ

2 4 6 8 10 9 7 5 3 1

© 2016 Jeannie Baker

The right of Jeannie Baker to be identified as author/illustrator of this work has been asserted
by her in accordance with the Copyright, Designs and Patents Act 1988

This book has been typeset in Humana Sans

The artwork was prepared as collage constructions which were reproduced
in full colour from colour photographs by Jaime Plaza

Image of globe on page 45 reproduced courtesy of Mountain High Maps©
Copyright © 1993 Digital Wisdom ©, Inc.

Printed in China

British Library Cataloguing in Publication Data:
a catalogue record for this book is available from the British Library

ISBN 978-1-4063-3801-0

www.walker.co.uk

www.walkerbooks.com.au

JEANNIE BAKER

Circle

In its lifetime a godwit may fly further
than from the Earth to the Moon and back.

WALKER BOOKS
AND SUBSIDIARIES
LONDON • BOSTON • SYDNEY • AUCKLAND

In a place where mud and sand become sea …

a godwit with white wing patches
flies up with his flock.

The moment is right
for the long journey north.

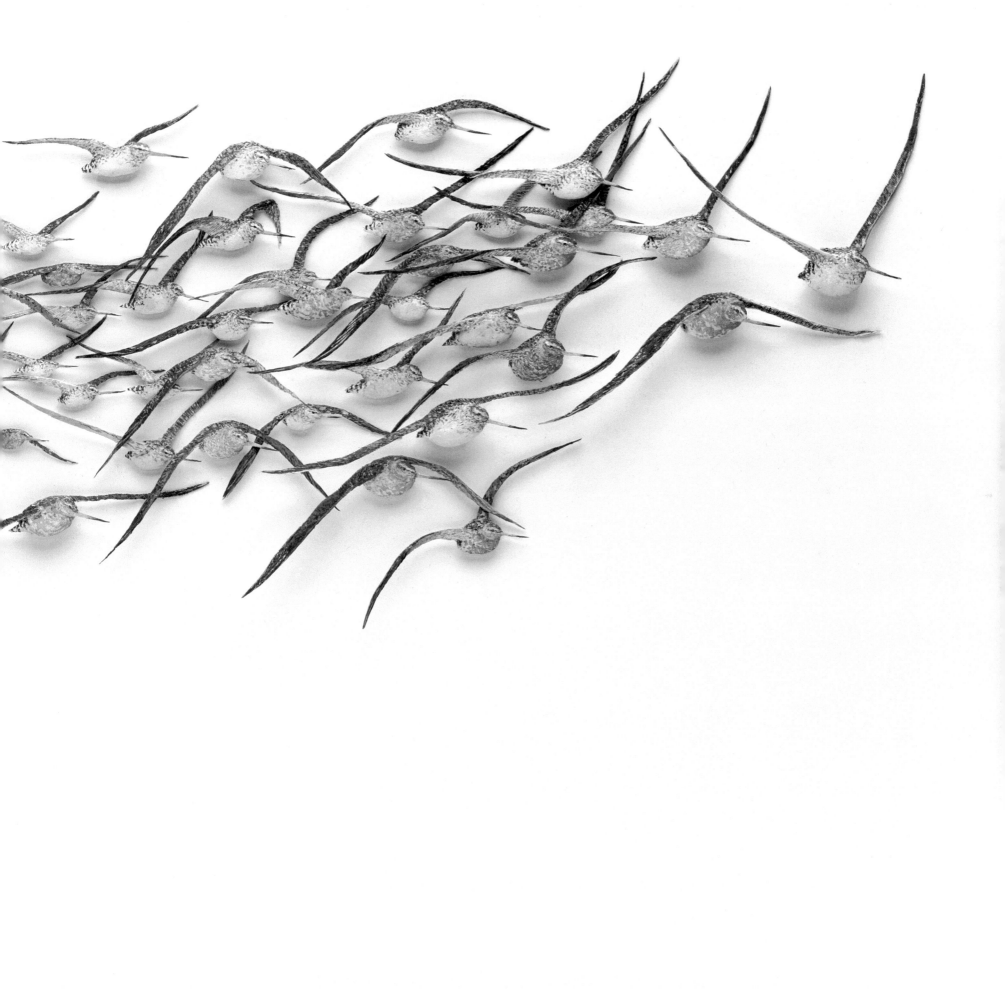

The flock fly high
above the clouds,
chattering at times
to help stay close together.
Each bird takes a turn
to lead the way.

They follow an ancient,
invisible pathway
for six nights
and six days,
until they know they need to stop.

The flock float down beneath the clouds,
each bird looking for food and somewhere safe to rest.
But the places they remember are gone.

They search in wider and wider circles.

Eventually the godwits find a safe stretch of mud.

At low tide the mud teems with food.
The godwit with white patches
eats day and night.

Days pass to weeks, still he eats,
until his body is swollen with fat
and it's time to move on ...

on with another flock ...

on and on …

following the ancient, invisible pathway
until they reach their northern home.

Now the godwit with white patches flies on alone,
back to his remembered place.

He scrapes a shallow nest
in the ground.

Awika-wika-wika-wikraaaaaaaaa-wika-wika-wik...

His singing rings across the land.
Dancing wildly through the air
in steep, twisting, graceful dives,
finally, he attracts a mate.

Soon the godwits guard
four perfect eggs, and then four
newly-hatched chicks,
taking it in turns to keep them warm.

A hungry fox finds the nest
and won't be stopped.

One chick hides,
crouched and still,
disappearing into
the colours of the land.

Weeks pass.

The chick is almost full-grown
and the godwits know it's time to move on.

The mother godwit leaves first.

The godwit with white patches goes next.

Their grown chick will follow later.

The godwits join other birds
at a feeding place on the shore.

The godwit with white patches
grows white and grey-brown feathers.
He becomes strong and fat.

But the days grow colder
and finding food is harder.

Late one afternoon,
when the wind is icy,
godwits call to each other.

The time is right.

Suddenly they leave as one.

Following an ancient, invisible pathway
high above the clouds,
each bird takes a turn to lead the way south.

Alone in an infinity of sky the tiny birds fly
on and on and on for nine nights and nine days,
without stopping …

until they reach the other side of the world.

The flock drop down beneath the clouds,
each bird searching for a safe place to settle.

The godwit with white wing patches
rests at last …

back in the place where mud and sand become sea.

Author's Note

The bar-tailed godwits (Limosa lapponica baueri) *in this story make the longest unbroken journey of any animal in the world. Before each Arctic winter they migrate 11,000 kilometres from their northern home in Alaska to their southern home in Australia and New Zealand, without even stopping to rest.*

On their return to the north, the godwits need to stop and feed in the wetlands of Southeast Asia, especially those around the Yellow Sea. Wetlands are important for migrating water birds as they provide areas where the birds can rest and find food, enabling them to complete their journeys. The Yellow Sea wetlands are rapidly disappearing as a result of land reclamation and development, and the godwits and other migrating shorebirds are finding it harder and harder to find places where they can rest and feed.

The annual movements across the world of millions of birds, sea creatures and other animals remind us that everything in nature is interdependent and connected. The changes we make on one side of the world can have consequences in another. The challenge we face now is how to live our lives without destroying the places that are crucial to the shorebirds' ancient, wondrous Circle of Life.

Jeannie Baker

For more information on godwits and shorebirds:
www.globalflywaynetwork.com.au
www.awsg.org.au
www.miranda-shorebird.org.nz

Godwit Migration Map

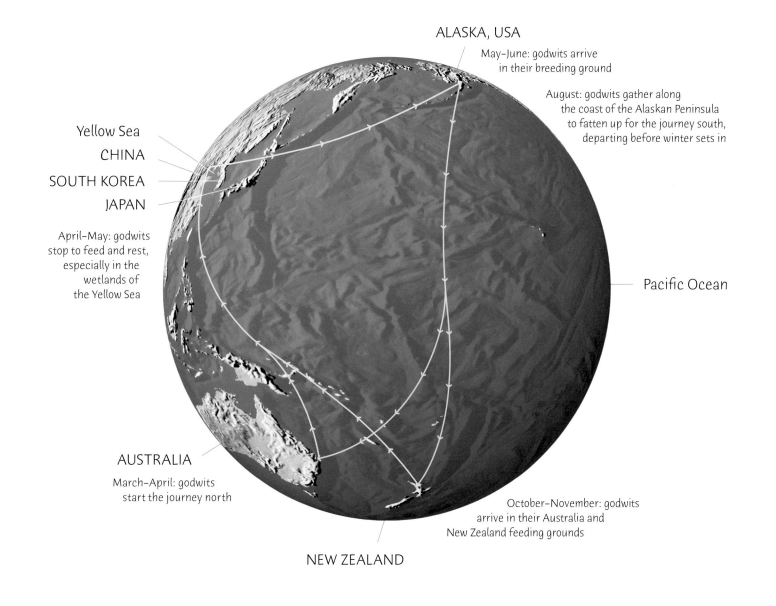

ALASKA, USA

May–June: godwits arrive
in their breeding ground

August: godwits gather along
the coast of the Alaskan Peninsula
to fatten up for the journey south,
departing before winter sets in

Yellow Sea

CHINA

SOUTH KOREA

JAPAN

April–May: godwits
stop to feed and rest,
especially in the
wetlands of
the Yellow Sea

Pacific Ocean

AUSTRALIA

March–April: godwits
start the journey north

October–November: godwits
arrive in their Australia and
New Zealand feeding grounds

NEW ZEALAND

Other migrating creatures in this book

Green turtles
Great knots
Arctic tern
Sandhill cranes
Brent geese
Caribou

Short-tailed albatross
Humpback whales
Curlew
Channel-billed cuckoo
Black-winged stilts